T0132384

MICHIGAN'S WESTERN U.P.

An Old Professor's Travel Guide of
Twenty-five Selected Locations
(Ironwood to Baraga)

RALPH G. PIFER

Archway Publishing books may be ordered through booksellers or by contacting:

Archway Publishing
1663 Liberty Drive
Bloomington, IN 47403
www.archwaypublishing.com
1 (888) 242-5904

Interior Image Credit: Ralph G. Pifer

Trail Along the Presque Isle River in the Porcupine Mountains
Late Fall—Driving Northward Near the Black River

ISBN: 978-1-4808-7980-5 (sc)
ISBN: 978-1-4808-7981-2 (e)

Print information available on the last page.

Archway Publishing rev. date: 01/02/2020

CONTENTS

WESTERN U.P. TRAVEL GUIDE PHOTO LISTING

INTRODUCTION

Welcome to Michigan's Western Upper Peninsula!

Travelers and explorers have been coming to Michigan's U.P. since prehistoric times. The first explorers were ancient Native Americans who came to mine copper for tools and trade. Many of their diggings became the great copper mines of the 1800s and early 1900s. The French brought the fur trade, exploring the wilderness, and trading with Native Americans. The British followed, building forts to protect settlers and the land for the king. In the 1800s and early 1900s, timbering, copper and iron mining, and fishing were major industries. Looking at the U.P.'s forests, it is hard to believe that they were almost totally lost to clear cutting and forest fires. It may be even harder to imagine the number of towns and villages that once existed. Near mines, timber operations, and along railroads, settlements sprung up. Complete with bars, stores, schools, churches, and even opera houses, they flourished briefly, dwindling, and then often totally disappearing when mining and logging ceased. Matchwood, Michigan was founded by The Diamond Match Company. Fire in 1893 almost destroyed it. Fire finished it in 1906. Mandan was a copper mining town with a population of 300 in 1910. Today, a few houses remain. Mandan's story is that of hundreds of mining towns. The land quickly reclaims man's abandoned works. There were more than 250 active copper mines in the U.P. during the 1800s and early 1900s. Today, they are one or two. The last major mine closed in 1995. The White Pine Mine was one of the largest underground mines in the world. Logging camps opened, then closed when the last tree was gone. The U.P.'s history is one of boom and bust. Tourism and logging are the main U.P. industries today. There is little heavy industry or manufacturing. The mines closed due to falling copper prices and labor strife. Less expensive open pit mining in the American West, and elsewhere, doomed them. Fishing was decimated by the lamprey eel. Lamprey control programs are gradually restoring fish stocks. Most of the U.P.'s great white pine forests are gone. Surprised? Transformed into matches, crates, and cheap lumber, they were not well managed. There is talk of reopening some mines, with rising copper prices and demand. Fishing has shown some recovery. Modern logging is more carefully managed.

The northern U.P. is dominated geographically and climactically by Lake Superior, the largest of the Great Lakes. Weather along the lake changes in minutes, from balmy and sunny to black skies, gusting winds, and heavy seas. The number of shipwrecks in Lake Superior is staggering, exceeding most salt water oceans. The Edmond Fitzgerald was one of the most famous victims of the U.P.'s changeable weather. Winters in the U.P. are long and cold, and snow is heavy, often exceeding several hundred inches. Winter comes early and leaves late. A friend quipped that there are 9 months of winter and 3 months of spring. Winter sports thrive, including skiing, snow shoeing, and ice fishing. Given the climate, agriculture is limited, but in recent years cattle production has been drawn by the potential for lush pasture land. Smoked fresh fish, fresh walleye, maple syrup, honey, grains and potatoes, and jams and jellies made from the many wild fruits available are the major products the land and water.

The Western U.P. consists of ancient volcanic mountain ranges that are billions of years old, among the oldest on earth. It is in these rocks that copper, iron, silver, gold, and traces of early life are found. Well worn, the mountains are more like rolling hills, but here and there, glimpses of their past glory are present. At the Porcupine Mountains State Park, looking down from the escarpment, there is a glimpse of that past. Skiing is big in the winter. Lake Superior's coast is often rocky, rugged, and is highly photogenic, though there are long sandy beaches too. In some areas, you can walk for hours along polished rock or long sand beaches. Watch for agates and other beautiful rock specimens. If the shore or mountains are not your cup of tea, there are over 12, 000 miles of rivers and streams, and over 4, 000 lakes. Canoeing and kayaking are possible on many of these bodies of water. Some, like the Presque Isle River, have far too many rapids and waterfalls to allow boating. Get your camera ready for these and be ready to hike some memorable trails overlooking them. Deep and soaring woods exist wherever you look and are criss-crossed by trails of varying difficulty. The Porcupine Mountains State Park has trails ranging in length from less than one hour to overnight. This park has 90 miles of hiking trails. The famous North Country Trail, which starts in New York State and stretches across the upper Midwest out to North Dakota, passes through the U.P. It is rugged, scenic, primitive, and takes hikers Porcupines waddle along roads.as are the O-Kun-de-Kun Falls.

If people are your thing, the U.P. may be the wrong place. You can find them, but the total population of the U.P. is a little over 300,000, or about 3% of Michigan's entire population. Large towns are few and far between. Marquette, the "largest town" in the Western U.P. has a population of 23,000. The three next largest Western U.P. cities are Houghton with 7,708, Iron Mountain, 7,624, and Ironwood with 5, 387. These are often sophisticated and very complete cities, but it can be a long ways between McDonald's, Walgreen's, or Casey's.

The animals of the U.P. include bear, deer, moose, bald eagles, porcupines, sandhill cranes, wolves, otters, and coyotes. Deer can be so common in the spring and fall as to be a driving hazard. Bears raid cabins, campsites, and cars where food is poorly stored. Wolves shoot across fields or pastures, or can be seen in the shadows, stalking their prey. Moose in river bottoms and swamps graze quietly. Eagles soar above the beaches, rivers, and lakes. Porcupines waddle along roads. If you are sharp eyed, you may see one in a tree top, munching leaves. If you are lucky, you may see an eagle carrying its prey. The U.P. is alive with wildlife. These are wild animals; use caution around them.

Finns, Italians, Cornish, Swedes, French-Canadians, and Native Americans make up most of the population. You will see their influence in names of roads, towns, and menu offerings—Toivola, Allouez, Ontonagon, Ahmeek, Lac La Bell, L'Anse, and pasties. Most were drawn by mining and logging. The unofficial slogan of the U.P. is the Finish word, "SISU." It means *to persist, to endure, to overcome adversity."* This slogan describes the population's hardscrabble history and their attitude toward the future. Life may be rugged here, but the arts and education are highly valued. You will encounter many arts and crafts studios in your explorations. Michigan Technological University, Finlandia University, and Gogebic Community College produce many of the nurses, medical technicians, social workers, mining engineers, artists, and law enforcement officers for the area. Finlandia and Northern Michigan Tech also draw a large number of students from around the world. It is not uncommon on a mine tour to be accompanied by engineering students from China, Japan, or Europe.

The people of the U.P. joke about tourists being carried off by mosquitoes, disappearing in clouds of black flies, having deer eat their gardens and wolves dine on their poodles. Do bring your insect repellent. Be ready for a Friday night fish fry. Have a pasty. Ski a slope. Try thimbleberry jam. Make chili from scratch on the shore of Lake Superior on a cool fall afternoon. Hike some trails; watch a sunset over Lake Superior; and shoot a lot of pictures! Hunt agates or visit a historic copper mine. There are endless things to see and do. Come on up!!! The air is fresh. The waters are clean. It is a different world.

"Nature is not a place to visit. It is home!!!!"   *—Gary Snyder*

Ontonagon River on a Foggy Morning

Young Buck with Velvet on his Antlers

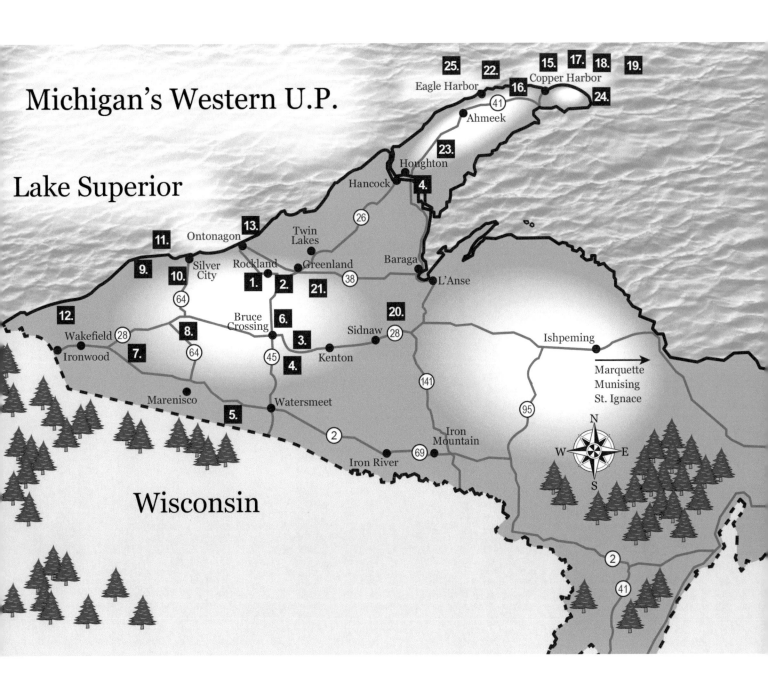

Michigan's Western U.P.

Lake Superior

Wisconsin

Carp River Valley in the Porcupine Mountains

TWENTY-FIVE SELECTED
WESTERN U.P. PLACES TO SEE

1 OLD VICTORIA: What was it like to be a copper miner in the 1800s or early 1900s? Mining was dirty, dangerous and hard work. Old Victoria is an original miner's settlement complete with Finnish sauna. Log cabins built by the miners are being restored. Several of the cabins are furnished as they would have been in 1900. There is a small fee to enter and look around in the buildings, but you can walk about the settlement and shoot pictures for free. Last time I was there, a table was covered with ancient rusted hardware, broken crockery, and glassware from excavations on the site. Old Victoria is officially open from Memorial Day until early fall. Your donations restore and maintain the site. **Driving directions**: In Rockland, just east of Henry's Bar, turn onto Victoria Dam Road, driving two miles south. The road goes through deep valleys, across several rivers, and past tall bluffs. I have shot some great fall pictures in this area. Old Victoria is on the right side of the road. Parking is along the road. The Victoria Mine and Victoria Dam are nearby. One of the most rugged and beautiful sections of the North Country Trail passes through the site. Not handicapped accessible.

2 Rockland Township Historical Museum: In 1900, Rockland and the area nearby had a population of hundreds. Rockland was a thriving mining town. There were multiple stores, bars, restaurants, and other businesses. Fine houses lined the streets. Today it is a fading shadow of its historical self. The Rockland Museum has a variety of artifacts from this period. Looking at Rockland today, you would never guess it was a busy and thriving settlement. Newspapers, photographs, and assorted artifacts describe the history of mining, agriculture, military, schools, and daily life in the area. A small donation is required. Driving directions: Drive south from Ontonagon on US-45 or north on US-45 from Bruce Crossing. Rockland is in the middle! The address is 40 National Ave. (US-45), Rockland, MI, 906-886-2821 or 906-886-2645.(GOOGLE for more information, hours, and cost.) The museum is in a former school building just outside the town driving south.

***Check Henry's Bar, in the middle of town, if you are hungry and have time, you will find great food and all sorts of information about the area.

3 AGATE FALLS: This is a spectacular waterfall on the Ontonagon River. The river was used during the heyday of logging in the U.P. to float logs downstream to saw mills. Imagine white pine logs, three feet or more in diameter and a hundred feet long, shooting over theses falls. **Driving directions: On M-28** drive roughly 4 miles west of Trout Creek. On the left side of the road is the Joseph E. Oravec Roadside Park. There is plenty of parking. Steep trails lead from the park down to the river. The temperature drops as you approach the mist from the falls. **It is a rugged climb down– EXERCISE CAUTION.** A viewing deck is available for the less adventurous. Toilet and picnic facilities are present. Not really handicapped accessible.

Restored Miner's Cabin at Old Victoria Mining Settlement

4 BOND FALLS: Bond Falls is almost unknown outside of Michigan. The falls are beautiful and have been voted the second best in Michigan (The best? Tahquamenon Falls.) Forty feet high and a hundred feet wide, the falls put on a great show in all seasons. They are framed by heavy forest on all sides, but a wide paved foot path from the parking area circles the base of the falls, allowing a variety of views—and camera angles. For those who are able, there are steep stairs on the right side of the falls to the top. There, the view is panoramic. You will be a few feet from the roaring water. Trees around the falls are spectacular in the fall. The falls are free! **Driving directions:** Take US-2 east out of Wakefield to Paulding, or US-45 south from Ontonagon to Paulding. Take Bond Falls Road 2.5 miles east from Paulding. Signs clearly mark the route to the park. The parking area is large. There are toilet facilities. Trails to the falls are not long and are handicapped accessible for wheelchairs and walkers. **KEEP AN EYE ON CHILDREN AT THE FALLS!**

5 SYLVANIA WILDERNESS: Believe it or not, most of the U.P. has been burned and logged off several times. Mining has also taken a toll. Before the arrival of European settlers, the U.P. was a breathtaking wilderness of glacial bogs, quiet clear lakes, eroded mountain ranges, and old growth forests. There were no cars, roads, or towns. The loon's cry could be heard. Eagles soared above the forest canopy. The sound of a pileated woodpecker or the call of a wolf could be heard through the woods. It was a wilderness– and still is, at the Sylvania Wilderness. Once the private reserve of the privileged few and American presidents, it is now a park you too can enjoy. **Driving directions:** If you are interested in deep quiet and unspoiled wilderness, go to the Ottawa National Forest Visitor's Center on County Road-535 off of US-2 west, out of Watersmeet. Here you can get information on camping, fishing, sightseeing, swimming, and other activities. There are very reasonable fees for day use or for the season—the latter is a good deal. The Ottawa National Forest Visitor Center is open from late May through mid October, 9 am until 5 pm. The Center has some nice displays of wildlife and plants in the park (906-358-4724). Vehicle use is extremely restricted in the park. Motors are not allowed on the lakes. Check the nearby **SYLVANIA OUTFITTERS**, 1 mile west of Watersmeet on US-2 (906-358-4766 or www.sylvaniaoutfitters.com) for information, kayaks, skis, boots, and canoe rentals. Accessibility varies throughout the park. Check with the Visitor's Center for areas that are.

"After you have exhausted what there is in business, politics, conviviality, and so on—have found none of these finally satisfy, or permanently wear—what remains? Nature remains!"

Walt Whitman

6 OKUN-DE-KUN FALLS (Also known as Baltimore Falls):It is a little over 1 mile from the trail head to the falls. The first hundred feet or so are boardwalk, then it becomes an earthen trail, with occasional boardwalks in wet areas. If the weather has been dry, the walk is not bad. If it has been a wet spring or is raining, it can be a very, very, wet and muddy hike. Ferns, streams, heavy woods, and wildflowers parallel the trail. The falls are not the biggest, but they are attractive. In wet periods, the falls flood over the banks and roar as they push through the channel. Be careful of getting too near the water during these periods. I have hiked to the O-KUN-DE-KUN Falls during dry and wet periods. Incidentally, the path to the falls is part of the famous NORTH COUNTRY TRAIL.

Bond Falls in the Summer, near Paulding, MI.

Sylvania Wilderness in Early Spring

🚗 **Driving Directions:** Take US-45 out of either Ontonagon and drive south about 20 miles—or drive north on US-45 from Bruce Crossing about 8 miles. North of the Baltimore River, you will see a pull-out and signage for O-KUN-DE-KUN-FALLS. Park in the lot at the pull-out. Not handicapped accessible. Oh—be sure to wear your bug repellent! Black flies and mosquitoes can be bad.

7 WOLF MOUNTAIN: This is not a place you will see or visit, unless you look for it. It is worth seeing! Ferns and wildflowers are common Along the path to the peak, depending upon the season. In the fall, the colors are memorable. The North Wood's quiet will strike you immediately when you turn off your engine. It may be a warm day when you arrive, but take along a sweatshirt or sweater for the peak. The wind on top can be cool. The path up is steep and can be slippery and muddy. Use caution. This is not a handicapped friendly site. It is strictly an unimproved trail. A stout walking stick will help. Be ready to pack out any trash you bring; there are no receptacles on the trail. Chances are you will be alone on your climb. The path to the top is shaded, opening to sunny spots and views. Arriving at the summit, the view will take your breath away. You can see for miles. Below is an ocean of trees. Bring a camera!!! This is a geat place for meditation or a picnic. Overnight camping is possible. It is not the Rockies, but it is worth the climb. Not handicapped accessible.

🚗 **Driving Directions:** Take U.S.-2 out of Wakefield; near Morenisco you will see Forest HWY 9300 or Wolf Mountain Road . It is a gravel road. The road sign is not large; you will have to look for it. The turnout is on the north side of the road. Drive north for roughly a mile on the road. The road ends in a turnabout; park along the edge of the road. A trail marker directs you to the top of the mountain.

"Heaven is under our feet as well as over our heads."   *Henry David Thoreau*

8 LAKE GOGEBIC AND LAKE GOGEBIC STATE PARK: Lake Gogebic is one of the largest lakes in Michigan, excluding the Great Lakes. It is also one of the best places in the state for walleye fishing. Yes—I know the jokes about walleye, but until you have had a deep fried walleye dinner, you have not lived!!! Camping, picnic areas, beaches, boat launches, playgrounds, showers and toilets are available. Recreation Passports* are needed for admission to some areas. These are some of the cleanest camping and picnic areas I have ever been in. There are private resorts, a general store, and some bars along the drive around the lake. The water in Lake Gogebic warms early because the lake is shallow. It is clean and clear. The hiking trails give you a good workout. The nearby towns of Bergland and Wakefield Have a couple of good restaurants, gas, and basic supplies.

🚗 **Driving Directions:** Take M-28 out of Wakefield to Merriweather (about 15 minutes), turn right onto M-65, the lake will be on your left for the next ten miles. Ahead, you will encounter LAKE GOGEBIC STATE PARK. There are a number of great waterfalls in the area and some lookouts too. Handicapped access varies from good to not accessible.

---

* GOOGLE the park and other state parks in Michigan for further information on the park and securing a Park Passport. For camping reservations, etc., call 906-842-3341.

View From Top Of Wolf Mountain

9 THE PORCUPINE MOUNTAINS STATE PARK:

The park has one of the largest stands of old timber east of the Mississippi. It has 60,000 total acres, 90 miles old virgin timber, 42 kilometers of groomed ski trails, and 30 waterfalls. The South Boundary Road, encompassing the southern flank of the park, is 27 miles long. The "Porkies" as they are affectionately known, are part of an ancient mountain range countless millions of years old. It is made up of towering ridges and deep broad valleys. Some of the hemlocks in the park are three feet across. Countless streams and rivers crisscross the park. The park has a number of ancient copper mining sites, as well as sites from the 1800s. Be sure to drive to the Lake of the Clouds Overlook. After a short hike to the viewing area, you will look over a broad valley, with Lake of the Clouds at the bottom. The lake is fed by the Big Carp River. The water is so clear you can see into the depths of the lake and river. Moose have been known to meander across the river. Bald eagles frequently soar over the deep valleys and ridges of the park. Bear wander along or across the park roads. Be careful of cubs in the summer and early fall. Trout are common in the lakes and streams.

There are many trails for hiking. Some are ideal for the day visitor; others challenge the serious trekker. Check with the park staff for suggestions. I have enjoyed the Pinkerton and Overlook trails. You can do the Pinkerton in an afternoon, passing through deep woods along cliffs, over a river, and finally coming out on Lake Superior. It is a great day hike. The Overlook Trail takes you along the ridge line of the Lake of the Clouds Valley. You are hundreds of feet above the valley floor and have great views. Stay on the trail. The Porkies are a place to spend several days or a week; if you only have one day, check out the Visitor's Center to learn about the park and its history. They will supply you with a state sticker and information on various places, maps, information about the best trails, camping, etc. There are also displays about the animals, geology, a massive topographical map of the park, a multimedia presentation on the Porkies, and a gift shop.

I have been visiting the U.P. since the 1970s. I have never tired of the Porkies* and always see and do something new. One the best meals I ever had in the U.P. was chili cooked from scratch over a campfire. I have watched a bear shepherd her three cubs across a road in a remote area. I have stood in the center of a woods of hundred foot white pines and hemlocks, soaking in the silence. It is a place that renews the spirit. *Be sure to have a camera with you!*

Driving Directions: There are several routes. Seventeen miles west from Ontonagon on M-107 will bring you to the park. Extensive signage will assist you. Another route involves taking M-26 from Ironwood to Bergland. At Bergland, turn north onto M-64. You will pass by White Pine. M-64 dead ends at Lake Superior; turn left on M-107. You will pass through Silver City. The park is less than ten miles away on this road. One can take County Road 519 outside of Wakefield northward until you encounter the South Boundary Road of the park. Take this road east and you will eventually (27 miles) come out at the park headquarters. <u>WARNING</u>—This road is not plowed if it snows. It may not be open from the first snow until May!! It is a dark road. You may encounter wildlife on this road at night. Consider exploring it in daylight. ***BE SURE TO HAVE LONG LASTING MAXIMUM STRENGTH BUG REPELLENT FOR BLACK FLIES IN THE SPRING***. Handicapped accessibility ranges from good to inaccessible. Check with the park for accessibility.

---

* Porkies—where did the name come from? Native Americans noticed that one of the peaks resembles the profile of a crouching porcupine.

Lake of the Clouds in the Porcupine Mountains - October

Bonanza Falls (aka Greenwood Falls) Late Summertime

10 BONANZA FALLS (Also known as Greenwoood Falls): The falls are over 100 feet wide and drop over multiple layers of rock. At one side, there is a deep pool that locals swim in during the summer. When the water is high, the falls can be spectacular. During dry periods, you can walk across the large sections of the falls. There are many great pictures to be had here in all seasons. A trail on the east bank of the river leads several miles through some beautiful heavily wooded areas above the river. North of the falls, about one mile, bald eagles nest and roost in some of the tall dead trees. In drier times, you can hike in the river bed, moving from rock to rock well up river. Though the site of silver mining at one time, nature has long ago erased those wounds. A picnic area and parking are available at the falls, but nothing more. It is not handicapped accessible.

🚗 **Driving Directions:** The falls are one mile south of Silver City on M-64. The turnout is clearly marked with signage. Further signage tells the history of the area, including the silver mining period. The falls are a few hundred feet beyond this.

11 UNION BAY: You don't have to go to Hawaii for a great beach. On your way to the Porcupine Mountains on M-106, you will drive past the white sand beach of Union Bay. The bay is several miles long, the water crystal clear, and the sand white and hard packed. The water and the beach are pristine. It is a great place for small and big kids to play in the waves on a hot summer day or to catch a few rays. The water will be cool even in the summer—this is Lake Superior! There are periodic turnouts where you can park. Many have grills. Sunsets are breathtaking on this stretch of beach. Be sure your camera is ready. Handicapped accessibility is limited.

🚗 **Driving Directions:** The beach is 15 miles west of Ontonagon on M-107 near the entrance to the Porcupine Mountains State Park.

12 BLACK RIVER WATERFALLS: This is a series of memorable waterfalls, each unique. Each is photogenic. The great northern woods takes your breath away as you walk through it. The quiet is broken only by the call of birds and the deep roar of the falls as you approach them. It is a place conducive to meditation and the contemplation of nature. It is not unusual to be the only person on a path. Looking about you, you realize how small man is in the nature.

🚗 **Driving Directions:** Take the Black River Road (County Road 513) out of Bessemer heading north. You will pass through Powder Horn Falls and by Big Powder Horn Mountain on your way. There will be signs pointing to the falls. Turnouts lead to parking areas, maps, and information about the falls and river. The trails to the falls will take you through old growth forests, over deep stream ravines, and through fern filled glens. Trails are ½ to 1.5 miles to the falls. Check at the trail head for exact distances. There are seven major falls and many lesser ones. Stairways lead down to viewing platforms at many of the sites. **DO NOT GET**

OFF THE PLATFORM OR IN THE RIVER. THESE ARE DANGEROUS WATERS. Some of the trails and stairs can be quite a workout—you will get your aerobic points for the day. Most are not handicap friendly. All the falls are contained in a two mile stretch. I shot some great fall color and U.P. waterfalls in October one year. Toilet facilities are present at the trail-heads. The falls are not handicapped accessible—or are with some difficulty.

13 ONTONAGON COUNTY HISTORICAL MUSEUM: This local museum is well worth the price of admission. It may not be Chicago's Field Museum, but it will help you understand the history and people of the area. The museum begins with the ancient Native Americans and moves to the present through a range of artifacts, photographs, and dioramas. While touring the museum some years ago, I saw pictures of the devastation from one of the several forest fires that have swept the U.P. Looking at Ontonagon, only a few chimneys and a bank vault were left standing. Everything else was ashes. A dentist's office, watch collection, harbor display, folk art, and antique musical instruments are a few of the things you will see. There are also major displays dealing with mining and logging. Both were once major industries of the area. Tours of the Ontonagon Light House are arranged at the museum. There is a reasonable fee. GOOGLE or call for information on hours and fees. The museum is accessible, but cluttered.

Driving Directions: 422 River Street, Ontonagon—906-884-6165— <ochs@jamadots.com>

14 A.E. SEAMAN MINERAL MUSEUM: *"WORLD CLASS"*—that is how this Houghton museum is best described. If you are a rock hound, geologist, or just interested in rocks and minerals, this is the place. The museum specializes in the minerals of Michigan, especially of the U.P. and the copper mining industry, but it has minerals from all over the world. There are thousands of breathtaking specimens in state of the art displays. The museum is the state mineral museum, combining the collections of Michigan Tech and the University of Michigan. Many private individuals have also contributed unique and outstanding specimens. The museum is a fantastic learning experience taking several hours at a minimum to see. Check the gift shop! They sell a variety of specimens, books, jewelry, and other goodies. Admission is well worth it.

Driving Directions: Take M-26 to Memorial Drive, which becomes College Drive (US-41) to MacInnes Drive. Turn right, driving 1.1 miles to the parking area of the museum. Signage points the way. 906-487-2572 <http://www.museum.mtu.edu/> Extensive information is online. Hours: 9 to 4:00 generally or GOOGLE for exact schedule. Handicapped accessible.

Copper Ore from Assorted U.P. Copper Mines

15 HUNTER'S POINT, COPPER HARBOR: This is a small gem, not to be missed. It is a crust of land on Lake Superior circling a clear bay on one side at Copper Harbor and facing Lake Superior on the other. Trails follow the shore, giving repeated memorable views of the bay and lake beyond that. Eventually, you come out on the rocky shore of Lake Superior. Huge rocks, cliffs, towering white pines, and views along the coast predominate. This is as good as it gets. All of this is 3.5 billion years old, made of some of the oldest rocks in the world. Wildflowers in season, eagles, hawks, and migrating birds are some of the animals you encounter. On the beach, you may find an agate. Read about the history of the place on the net. It was saved from developers by the locals and is an excellent example of social action. Donations to aid in the preservation and care of the park are gratefully accepted.

Driving Directions: Take M-26 northward along Lake Superior to Copper Harbor. You hug the Lake Superior shoreline much of the time, passing by great scenery and through a number of interesting small towns. Jam, antiques, and a monastery are along the way. On the outskirts of Copper Harbor, turn left at North Coast Shores or continue on to the marina on M-26 where you will find parking and a scenic trail to Hunter's Point. Take the first turn on North Coast Shores to the right on Harbor Coast Lane to Hunter's Point where you will find parking, restrooms, and a handicapped access point. At the Marina, park in the general parking. The trail is clearly marked on the south side of the parking area. If it is spring or has been raining, it can be muddy and waterlogged in spots. Wear appropriate footwear. Be sure to have a camera. You can use the facilities at the Marina or at the entrance off North Coast Drive. Check the Marina's gift shop if you park there. The boat for Isle Royale leaves from here! Hunter's Point, P.O. Box 76, Copper Harbor, MI. 49918. Phone 906-289-4292 < www.hunters-point.org/index.html> The trail is partially handicapped accessible, with a viewing stand looking over Lake Superior. The handicapped area is at the Coast Lane site.

"An early morning walk is a blessing for the whole day."　　　　　　　*–Henry David Thoreau*

16 BROCKWAY MOUNTAIN DRIVE: Who says getting high is illegal?? Brockway Drive follows a ridge top for some miles. It is the highest road between the Rockies and Alleghenies! You look northward to Copper Harbor, Lake Fanny Hoe, and Lake Superior. Off to the east is a deep forested valley between ridge lines. To the west, is Lake Superior. You may see ore carriers heading north or south on the lake. To the south is a series of lakes. I have watched storms building on Lake Superior and moving inland from atop the ridge. There are a number of trails and places to visit. On one occasion, I sat in my car eating cold, leftover Chinese food while I watched a storm build and sweep in. The drive up is great; the drive down is just as good. While the trails are not handicapped accessible, most of the best sights are visible from a car.

Driving Directions: Entrances to Brockway Ridge Road are on M-26. One is five miles northeast of Eagle Harbor on M-26 on the right side of the road. It is clearly marked. The other entrance is ½ mile west of Copper Harbor on M-26. It is clearly marked. There is no charge. **Be aware, this road is not plowed from the first snow until May, when it melts.**

17 FORT WILKINS STATE PARK: Want to visit a frontier fort as it was in the 1800s? Fort Wilkins looks like it dropped out of the sky in the 1800s and landed in the U.P. You will touch, see, and live history here. It is one of the best preserved instances of the architecture and lifestyle of this period in U.S. history. The fort was built in 1846 to protect miners and bring law and order to the wilderness. Some historians have suggested that the fort was built to protect the Native Americans from the miners! It was occupied briefly before being abandoned; then used as a local picnic area before being made into a park. Restoration started in the 20th century. The fort is almost exactly as it was when open. Archeological digs and restoration efforts have produced a site where history lives. A Cannon waits to be fired; a blacksmith shop could produce horseshoes and a bakery could bake fresh bread and rolls. There are officers' quarters, a powder magazine, a brig, enlisted mens' quarters, parade grounds, warehouses, and other structures. Historical re-enactors drill, dance, fire the cannon, and re-create life as it would have been at the fort. There are also ancient copper mines next to the fort. And—the fort is on the shore of "Lake Fanny Hooe." The name is real and there is quite a story behind it. I will let you discover that. Picnic areas, trails for hiking, ski trails, fishing, a children s' playground, a gift shop, camping, and toilets are available.

Driving Directions: The park is 1.5 miles east of Copper Harbor on M-41. It is on the right side of the road and hard to miss. There is extensive signage. Call 906-289-4215 or GOOGLE for more information. Or, you can write to: Fort Wilkins Historic State Park, P.O. Box 71, Copper Harbor, MI 49918. It is handicapped accessible to some goodly degree.

18 KEWEENAW MOUNTIN LODGE AND GOLF COURSE: Golf anyone? Dinner? Martinis? Overnight in a log cabin? In the depths of the Great Depression, President Roosevelt's Works Progress Administration (WPA) fought unemployment by putting people to work building parks, roads, post offices, and other projects. The Keweenaw Mountain Lodge and Golf Course was one of the projects. Workers cleared 167 acres of heavily timbered rocky ground. They saved the massive white pine logs and used them to build the lodge and cabins. When they were done, they had built a beautiful massive lodge, a series of cabins, and a nine hole golf course. Today all these things remain—as well as bike trails, shuffleboard, and tennis. I had one of the best charbroiled pork steak dinners I can ever remember. The steak was huge, the salad great, and the wild rice, tender. A corner of heaven!

Driving Directions: Take M-26 out of Eagle River and drive into Copper Harbor. Turn right onto U.S.-41 south at the junction of M-26 and U.S.-41. Take U.S. 41 for about one mile; the lodge and golf course will be very visible. You can also take U.S.-41 north from Hancock to the Lodge—the lodge will be outside of Copper Harbor on the right. Call 906-289-4403 or GOOGLE for further information. Handicapped- accessible, to some goodly degree.

19 HORSESHOE HARBOR—NATURE CONSERVANCY'S MARY MACDONALD PRESERVE: This attraction is a Nature Conservancy Site called the Mary MacDonald Preserve. It is the largest bedrock beach preserve in the state. The rocks are at least one billion years old. They contain some of the oldest fossils in the world. Many of the preserve's plants are more common to the Pacific Northwest

Enlisted Men's Quarters at Fort Wilkins near Copper Harbor

than to the Midwest. Some are extremely rare. As you walk from the parking area, you will encounter trees hung with long strands of greyish lichen. Bear, eagles, peregrine falcons, snowshoe hare, and deer roam the preserve. The harbor is rocky and deep. It is framed on one side by a conglomerate/sandstone dike and on the other by rocky cliffs. As you get closer to the lake, the air temperature begins to fall and you start to hear the roar of waves on the beach. Sitting on the beach, I have watched massive ore freighters slide by in deep water beyond the harbor's rocky reef. Kayakers paddle in from the rough lake to the quiet bay. You look at fossils hundreds of millions year old. The bay is a quiet and eternal place in the larger chaos of the world.

Driving Directions: Take US-41 north through Copper Harbor, past Fort Wilkins to where the blacktop ends. Continue east on the dirt road about one mile; watch for signage on the left. Turn left onto a dirt and sand road for about 1.2 miles. Drive carefully—the sand can be deep and if the weather has been wet, there can be mud and water. Parking is along the road. From the trail head to the harbor is about a half mile hike. GOOGLE the site for further information. Not handicapped accessible. Take pictures, explore, enjoy, take nothing, and please carry out your trash.

20 STURGEON RIVER GORGE: There are drives that are adventures. This is one. Canyons and gorges of this river system are as deep as 300 feet. They were formed by the action of the Sturgeon and Little Silver Rivers cutting through solid rock. Once you arrive at the river valley, you will never be far from the river, as you drive through heavy woods. The river is clear, rushing through and over rocks. There are 6,735 acres in this wilderness. Bear and deer are common. Kayaking and canoeing are possible, but only recommended for advanced white water experts. The attractive Sturgeon Falls are on this road, but a very difficult climb down to access. Silver Mountain is nearby. It may be worth a detour and climb to the top. Also, be sure to stop at the "Bear's Den" lookout point. You will get a scenic view that is breathtaking. The Sturgeon River Gorge can be a long and rough drive. Do not undertake it, unless your vehicle is in good shape, preferably all wheel or four wheel drive, and you have studied the route. If it has been a wet spring or rainy summer, there will be deep mud and water in spots. Fishing is generally poor on this river stretch, but photography is great!!!

Driving Directions: Take M-28 from Bruce Crossing to Sidnaw. Just through Sidnaw, take Pequet Lake Road north to Sturgeon Gorge Road. Stay on Sturgeon Road until it becomes Forest Road 193. Stay on this until it becomes NF 2270; stay on this until you run into Prickett-Dam Road. This will take you to M-38. Left will take you back to Ontonagon. Right will take you to Baraga. Start early in the day for this adventure! Be equipped. GOOGLE for more information and maps, and be sure to have a map with you.

"In the wilderness is the preservation of the world."   *Henry David Thoreau*

Turtle Looking about Before Diving

21 THE ADVENTURE MINE: This is a family owned operation in Greenland, Michigan. It is a historic mine site, first mined by Native Americans approximately 5,000 years ago. The Adventure Mine opened in 1850 and had extensive underground workings and above ground buildings, but was never profitable, despite the presence of a great deal of very pure copper. Poor management doomed the mine. It would close in 1920, though it would be worked by tribute miners periodically after that. The above ground structures were torn down and the machinery salvaged. A few years ago, the site was bought, roads cut, the shafts pumped dry, and improvements made to make the site accessible. This is a very typical mine of the period. The staff offer short tours underground of little more than one hour, up to tours that last an entire morning or afternoon. You will learn more about mining and copper mining specifically than you can imagine. I learned to rappel down a rock face to take the "Captain's Tour" one afternoon. Some areas of the mine have not been visited for over 100 years. Candles that lit the work are still in place. Shovels lean against the walls, and have for 100 years. Rails and ore cars are in place, waiting for use. Masses of copper hang from the walls and tunnel ceilings waiting to be brought to the surface. The staff will provide you with a helmet, light, and guide. Wear heavy boots or shoes, a light coat, and clothes you do not mind getting wet and muddy. It is cool (48 degrees) underground even in the middle of summer. Ice filled some of the deeper reaches of the mine when I toured. The mine grounds have a gift shop, camping and picnic sites, extensive bike paths, and a variety of other activities. Great place. Nice people. The mine opens in May and is usually open into October.

Driving Directions: Take M-38 southeast out of Ontonagon to Greenland. Thirteen miles and you will see signage on M-38 that will direct you where to turn off for the mine. Take 200 Adventure Ave. Signs on this road will lead you to the mine office and other attractions. 906-883-3371. Check the website for tour details, hours, and other information. <info@ adventureminetours.com> Not handicapped accessible.

—Modern mining extracted 11 billion tons of copper in the U.P. before mining ended.

22 THE GREAT SAND BAY: Life is a beach—at The Great Sand Bay in the Keweenaw Peninsula. It is a white sand, wave washed, gravel beach that curves inward from Lake Superior. There are a number of turnouts where you can look out over the lake and watch massive ore carriers following the coast downward to Minnesota. You are on a ridge several hundred feet above the beach. Behind you on the other side of M-26, sand dunes stretch. Wooden stairs take you down to the beach. Even on a cool day, the sand is warm. You are in the Keweenaw Peninsula heading north to the most northern part of Michigan—and here is a warm, wide beach. Oh—keep your eyes open for an agate. The lake washes and changes the rocks and sand along the shore constantly, uncovering and depositing agates.

Driving Directions: Drive up M-26, and between Eagle River and Eagle Harbor, you will encounter The Great Sand Bay.

Late May Snow Near Greenland, MI.

Agate Collectors at Great Sand Bay near Eagle Harbor, MI.

23 HOUGHTON COUNTY MUSEUM: The museum is located in the former smelter office and medical dispensary of the historic Calumet and Hecla Mining Company. There are three stories of exhibits. In addition, the museum campus consists of a one room school house, rail depot, log cabin, ruins of smelters, ore crushing mills, and the Perl Merrill Research Center among other things. Be sure to ride on the Lake Linden & Torch Lake Railroad train that circles the grounds, pulled by a restored Porter Steam engine. The engine gives tours, but once was used to transport mill and smelter material for the Calumet & Hecla Mine. You can listen to the sound of the old steam engine and feel the jolt of the car you sit in as it picks up speed and begins to move. The complex has exhibits dealing with the mines and mining in the area. It also explores what life would have been like during this period, with a variety of artifacts from the area including the area's first x-ray machine, dental equipment, the company pharmacy, and a beer wagon. Many of these are in rooms recreating shops, businesses, and homes of the early 20th century U.P. mining community. There is a lot to learn and see here. Plan to spend more than an hour and be delighted with all that you see.

Driving Directions: Drive on M-26 northward from Hancock, to south of Lake Linden. Large signage marks the extensive museum campus. Parts of the campus, such as the genealogical center, are open year round. The rest is open various hours starting in June through September. Call ahead for hours. 906-296-4121 or GOOGLE for extensive information on the site. Handicapped accessible to some goodly degree.

24 ESTIVANT PINES: Before man, Logging, mining, and forest fires, what did the U.P. look like? How tall were the white pines and other great trees? What was it like to walk through the great Northern woods? Estivant Pines is among the last stands of virgin white pine in the U.P. It takes up 508 acres above Copper Harbor. White pines are 130 to 150 feet tall and some 600 years old. There are 85 different bird species, 10 orchid species, and 256 plant species in total, including bloodroot, anemones, sarsparilla, violets, pyrolas, asters, and many others. Bear, coyotes, wolves, and many other large species roam the sanctuary. Be sure to have your camera and hiking boots for this site. Trails of 1, 1.2, and 2.5 miles wind through the sanctuary, giving great views of the trees. The terrain is rugged. Be prepared for a vigorous hike. No hunting, trapping, fishing, fires, camping, or motor vehicles are allowed. Please carry out all trash.

Driving Directions: Drive on M-26 from Calumet and through Copper Harbor to Manganese Road. Turn right on Manganese Road and drive to Burma Road. Signage will direct you to Estivant Pines. These are clay and gravel roads. Mud can be deep. If it has been raining or a wet spring, it is advisable to have an all-wheel or four wheel drive. Limited parking is available at the site. You may be the only person or group on the trails. This is a place of great solitude, where one is very close to nature. Not handicapped accessible.

25 EAGLE HARBOR LIGHTHOUSE AND MUSEUMS: The Eagle Harbor Lighthouse is a beautiful example of a late 1800s red brick lighthouse. The keeper's quarters are restored as they would have been in the 1930s. You step back in time as you walk through the kitchen, parlor, and other rooms. The great light's care and history are explored in detail. Today, the lighthouse is an automated working facility.

Trail at Estivant Pines above Copper Harbor, MI.

St. John's Monastery Near Eagle Harbor, MI.

The museum campus not only explores the lighthouse's history, but also the various notable shipwrecks in the area. The bay has a rocky, narrow opening, and there are many shoals off the shore. Relics and pictures detail the triumph and tragedy of the wrecks. There is also a commercial fishing museum, among others. The museum complex also tells the history of the local area—prehistoric copper mining, the notable local figures, Copper Harbor, and a variety of other topics. This is a fantastic resource if you are interested in the history of the area. Plan to spend some hours here. This is not a place to run through.

Driving Directions: Take M-26 from Hancock northward to Eagle Harbor. As you enter the village, you will see signage leading to the lighthouse. M-26 goes right around the bay and northward. Stay left, following the signage; it will take you to the lighthouse's parking lot. The lighthouse and museums are open from Mid-June through September. GOOGLE for hours. A small entry fee is required. You may photograph the exterior of the lighthouse for free. Not really handicapped accessible.

—*Did you know that Lake Superior is considered by most sailors as more dangerous than the world's oceans?*
—*Did you know that there are more shipwrecks in Lake Superior than in most oceans?*

BONUS SITES TO VISIT

If you liked the previous twenty-five destinations, check out the following five bonus sites.

1 COPPER TOWN USA MUSEUM IN CALUMET: One person reviewing this site said that it was not the largest museum, but that it had a heck of a lot to see! This Calumet museum explores almost all aspects of copper mining in the U.P., from prehistoric mining to the heyday of U.P. copper mining. Exhibits include mining machinery, tools, clothes, minerals, a mine office, the surgery from an actual mine, and many more items. This is a favorite place to visit. You get a very good insight into the life of the minders and their daily work world. The museum also has exhibits dealing with major local historical events, such as the Italian Hall Tragedy (massacre), where 73 people, mostly children, died when someone shouted "Fire", during a crowded Christmas celebration. Most were crushed to death in the resulting stampede. New exhibits are always being developed. There is a small entry charge. This museum is only open from June through September. GOOGLE the site for specifics on charges, hours, and other information.

Driving Directions: Take Route #41 out of Hancock, northward to Calumet. The museum is at 25815 Red Jacket Road in Calumet. There is good signage leading to the museum. It is fairly accessible for all ages.

2 HUNGARIAN FALLS IN HUBBELL: This is a hidden gem of a waterfall along a deep gorge. Great hiking, climbing, and picture-taking opportunities abound at this site. While the Hungarian River has been dammed, it drops over a series of cliffs and into deep gorges as it heads toward Torch Lake. Supervise children carefully!!! **If you are not in top shape, or cannot walk distances, do not visit this site.** It may take a little searching to find it.

Driving Directions: When you cross the drawbridge at Houghton heading toward Hancock, turn right immediately onto Royce Road/M-26. Head for Hubbell; continue on M-26 northward to 6th Street in Hubbell. Turn left and drive until you see a sign for a golf course. Watch for signs and trails on the left side of the road over the next ½ mile. Park along the road; stay on the marked trails. There are many side trails that may get you lost. Depending upon your physical condition, this hike may take several hours. *Not recommended for handicapped, elderly, or young explorers.*

Late Day Sunset Over Lake Superior near Silver City

3 BARAGA COUNTY HISTORICAL MUSEUM: This small museum tells the history of Baraga, Michigan and surrounding areas – and there is a lot of it! Exhibits start with Captain James Bendry, the founder of Baraga, and move to the recent past and present with a variety of marine artifacts. There is an emphasis on the Native Americans of the area, tools of the period, the logging industry, and mining. Clothes, personal possessions, the trappings of daily life, and records of births, deaths, and marriages, are a few of the items in the collection. Baraga is rich in history and much of it can be found in this small museum.

Driving Directions: Look for an attractive log cabin (This is it!) on U.S.41, as you head south around the bay. The museum is just north of the Best Western Lakeside Inn. It is open from June through September, Monday through Saturday, 11 until 3:00 p.m. There is a small entrance fee. The museum and grounds are handicapped accessible. GOOGLE for more information.

4 PRESQUE ISLE RIVER TRAIL IN THE PORCUPINE MOUNTAIN'S PARK: The Porcupine Mountains State Park has already been mentioned. One of the most scenic hikes, with multiple scenic waterfalls and other vistas, is along the Presque Isle River. The hike is several miles long paralleling the river, sometimes taking one to the edge of the shore. It is a challenging hike through heavy woods consisting of ancient white pines, hemlocks, and other magnificent trees. One can hike on either the east or west side of the river, eventually coming out at Lake Superior. The west side has some easier access for the handicapped and those not in great hiking condition. The east side is an up and down climb along a largely undeveloped trail. Both sides offer the hiker memorable views. Be sure to have your camera with you! There are five major waterfalls along this trail: Iagoo Falls; Unnamed Falls; Manabezho Falls; Manido Falls, and Nawadaha Falls. These are the named ones; there are countless smaller rapids that remain unnamed. The western side of the river trail ends at a swinging bridge that soars over roaring waters, passing through a narrow, potholed gorge on the way to Lake Superior. The bridge is a great place from which to shoot pictures. It leads over to Presque Isle, a forested island on the edge of Lake Superior.

Driving Directions: There are several ways to get to this trail. One can take R #28 out of Ironwood, through Bessemer and Wakefield, to County Road #519; turn left on this beautiful deep woods road and stay on it until you arrive at South Boundary Road in Porcupine Mountains State Park. Turn right, drive 50 feet, and park alongside the road near the bridge over the Presque Isle River. You will see the trails on either side of the bridge on the north side of the road. One can also take R #107 out of Silver City to the Boundary Road at the Porcupine Mountains State Park. Make a left onto the Boundary Road from R #107 and drive roughly 27 miles. The road will cross the Presque Isle River—you are there! *Be aware that the Boundary Road is a "seasonal" road, not plowed until May. Snow can come in early October and late May in the U.P.* GOOGLE the park site for current information on handicapped access. You will need a Michigan day pass or seasonal park pass to explore this site, purchasable at the park headquarters.

Eagle Harbor Lighthouse

5 THE HANKA HOMESTEAD MUSEUM: In the late 1800s, the Hanka family from Finland settled on the only road from the Keweenaw Bay, westward. The homestead would serve as home to the Hanka family for 70 years. The farm-homestead is representative of many Finnish farms and settlements of the time. Life as it was, during this period, is preserved in the farmhouse, barns, milk house, sauna, and outbuildings, the latter made of hand-hewn logs. The Hankas raised chickens and milk cows and grew vegetables and grains, as well as tanning hides. The preservation and restoration of the homestead is frozen in time, as it was in 1920. The Hankas generally did not adopt newer technology. The last family member died in 1960. The homestead is open from Memorial Day into the fall color season. Tours during this period can be arranged. GOOGLE the museum site for information on hours and dates.

Driving Directions: Take R #41 north, out of Baraga for about ten miles, heading for Chassell and Houghton. At Arnheim Road, turn left. The homestead is deep in the country; wooden signs point the way. Handicapped accessibility is limited. There is a modest entry fee. It is advisable to contact the site before making the rather long drive, to check if it is open and the hours of business.

NEED HELP?????????????????????

(Law Enforcement)

<u>BARAGA COUNTY</u>—Baraga, L'Anse, Assins, Skanee
SHERIFF: 906-524-6177
STATE POLICE: 906-524-6121

<u>GOGEBIC COUNTY</u>—Bessemer, Ironwood, Wakefield, Watersmeet
SHERIFF: 906-667-0203

<u>HOUGHTON COUNTY</u>—Calumet, Chassel, Donken, Copper City, Kearsarge, Laurium, Hancock, Houghton, Painesdale, South Range, Toivola, Trimountain, Twin Lakes, Winona
SHERIFF: 906-482-0055

<u>IRON COUNTY</u>—Alpha, Amasa, Beechwood, Caspian, Crystal Falls, Iron River
SHERIFF: 906-875-0650

<u>MARQUETTE COUNTY</u>—Marquette, Big Bay, Champion, Gwinn, Ishpeming, Skandia, Negaunee, Michigamme, Huron Mountain
SHERIFF: 906-643-1911
STATE POLICE: 906-475-9922

<u>ONTONAGON COUNTY</u>—Bergland, Bruce Crossing, Ewen, Greenland, Lake Gogebic, Mass City, Victoria, Rockland, Paulding, White pine, etc.
SHERIFF: 906-884-4901

NEED MEDICAL CARE????????????

Medical emergencies happen. One can fall while hiking, burn a hand while cooking at a campfire, or get caught in your own fishing line. Illness does not always wait until you get home. The medical care I have received in the U.P. has always been prompt and top drawer.

The following are sources of medical care:

IRONWOOD AREA
Aspirus Grand View Hospital   906-524-7156
U.S. #2, Ironwood, MI.

ONTONAGON AREA
Aspirus Ontonagon Hospital   906-884-8000
601 S. 7th St., Ontonagon, MI.

BARAGA AREA:
Baraga County Memorial Hospital   906-524-3300
18341 US Hwy 41, L'Anse, MI.

HOUGHTON-HANCOCK-PORTAGE AREA
Aspirus Houghton Clinic   906-487-1710
1000 Cedar Street, Houghton, MI.

U.P. Health System—Portage Express Care   906-483-1777
921 Sharon Ave.
Houghton, MI.

U.P. Health System—Portage Main Campus   906-483-1000
500 Campus Dr.
Hancock, MI.

Sandhill Crane

UPPER PENINSULA SAFE TRAVEL TIPS

— Keep your gas tank full; it can be a long time (and walk!) between gas stations.

— If you're traveling back roads, logging or mining roads, or off road, have the following items with you: shovel, saw, blanket, water, and jumper cables. –Why a saw? Trees fall across roads; I once helped six other people cut up a tree so we could pass.

— Be aware the secondary roads are not plowed from first snow until May—a long wait.

— Let someone know where you will be, if you are going to be somewhere remote or off-road.

— Cell phones do not work, or work reliably, in many areas of the U.P.

— Do not feed the animals. Bears will rip a window out of car for a bag of donuts.

— Have cash on hand; there may not be an ATM handy.

— Be sure you have a good map; your GPS, like a cell phone, may not work.

— Have plenty of film or extra SD cards for your camera—and an extra camera. I once had to buy a new camera when my old one died.

— Have a first aid kit.

— Do not wade or swim at waterfalls. Dangerous currents, whirlpools, and underwater hazards are common. People have died wading and swimming in these places.

— Beware of poison ivy at old mine sites; it loves to grow in mine dumps.

— Black flies are a real problem in the spring. Bring and use DEET containing repellants. Zinc oxide (diaper rash cream) dries the bites up. Ticks and mosquitoes become a problem later in the season.

— Dress in layers. It may be 30 degrees in the morning, 60 by noon, and 80 by mid-afternoon. Wear SERIOUS shoes or hiking boots. Flip flops are not good in mud, snow, or icy water. They also are not safe on rocky ground or in mines.

— Weather changes rapidly in the U.P. It can—and does snow in mid-May and early October. Be prepared; check the forecast. Storms can come up very fast.

— Store and attraction hours can be quirky. Many things are only open from Memorial Day until Labor Day. Check ahead via GOOGLE or phone for open times.

— Make reservations. It is an awful feeling to drive for hours, only to find the hotel/motel you were counting on is closed or full; and

— HAVE FUN, TAKE PICTURES, BE SAFE, AND COME BACK!!!!

After the Storm Along Lake Superior's Shore

HELPFUL U.P. TRAVEL AND HIKING PUBLICATIONS

50 Hikes in Michigan's Upper Peninsula by Thomas Funke, The Countryman Press.
This book describes hikes of varying lengths and difficulty. It has excellent maps, with good detail. Instructions for getting to the hiking areas are clear. The book also covers what to look for on the hikes.

Gentle Hikes of Upper Michigan by LaDonna Tornabene, Lisa Voelsang, and Melanie Morgan, Adventure Publications.
If you are a hiker, this is the best resource for planning day hikes to a variety of sites. Instructions and maps are clear. Information on public sites and special needs are included.

Hiking Michigan. 2nd ed. by Roger Storm and Susan Wedzel, Human Kinetics Press.
Large, easy to read book, with great maps—146 day hikes with good detail about what you will see and associated points of interest.

Hunt's Guide to Michigan's Upper Peninsula. 2nd ed., By Mary Hunt and Don Hunt, Midwestern Guides.
This is a great guide, but has not been updated in sometime and is getting a little long in the tooth. Some businesses listed have closed and new ones opened. It has a very good index of sites to visit, lists of sites by geographic areas, and is loaded with excellent descriptions of sites, drawings, and black and white pictures.

Lake Superior Magazine and Travel Guide 1-888-BIG-LAKE or www.LakeSuperior.com
This magazine of the travel guide is a good source of current information about the Lake Superior area, including the U.P. It is loaded with color pictures, reviews, easy to read maps, and solid information. Ads in the magazine list hotels and businesses that may be of interest. Articles spotlight people, events, and places that are unique to the area.

Michigan: An Explorer's Guide 2008, Jeff Counts, **Countryman Press**
This book covers the entire state of Michigan, but the best part of 100 pages is devoted to the U.P. It hits the highlights.

Michigan State Parks: A Complete Recreation Guide. 2nd ed., The Mountaineers Press
This book covers all the parks of the U.P. It provides a lot of useful detail. It has maps of the parks and park contact information.

Michigan's Upper Pernsinsula—Great Destinations A Complete Guide. By Amy Westervelt, The Countryman Press
This a solid black and white guide to the U.P. There are good maps, black and white pictures, and descriptions of popular places. The book is broken into a number of major geographic areas and covers history and getting around in the U.P.

Moon's Michigan Upper Peninsula. 3rd ed., by Paul Vachon, Avon Travel
A good detailed travel guide to Michigan's U.P. This covers almost every aspect of a trip. It has been around for awhile and has a good track record of guiding travelers.

Pure Michigan—official travel and tourism website for Michigan
http://www.michigan.org
This in many ways is the most detailed last word on whatever you want to know about travel in Michigan. Colorful, up to date, detailed, easy to use, it is always worth checking for information before a trip.

Walking Paths & Protected Areas of the Keweenaw, Editor Joan Chadde, Michigan Nature Assoc.
This small book focuses only on the Keweenaw Peninsula in the U.P. The book covers 22 main hikes and a number of lesser ones. Maps, travel directions to the site, a description of the site, and what you will see, are present. Hikes are rated by difficulty; pay attention to this information. Some of these hikes are real workouts. Many of the trails take you into wild and largely unspoiled areas. Be prepared!

Hunter's Point near Copper Harbor, MI

ACKNOWLEDGEMENTS AND THANKS

The writing of this book would not have been possible without the assistance of the following people and organizations. Much is owed to them for their assistance and friendship over the last forty years. They represent the very best of Michigan's U.P.

Bill and Gladys for introducing me to the U.P. forty years ago. Linda for bringing me back to the U.P. and enjoying it with me. Elaine for putting up with all my expeditions, photo taking, and rock collecting. Jackie McMullen who became a good friend and made many suggestions about my photography. Julie Chasca and the staff at the Porcupine Mountains AmericInn who for thirty years have made me feel like family and helped me through a broken shoulder and a heart attack. Also, many thanks for cleaning up all the sand I have tracked in, tolerating my specimens lining your windowsills, and keeping my room fresh and clean. Special thanks to Mary Shegan who suggested I write this book and helped with the preparation of the first edition. Ontonagon Memorial Hospital's Emergency Room's excellent professional staff who patched me up over the years, giving me the best of care. Ariel and Ashley who reviewed thousands of pictures making suggestions for their use. Antonio's, who have fed me countless lunches and dinners. The members of the Settler's Depot and Gallery at Bruce Crossing who gave my photography a home and encouraged me in the writing of this book deserve special thanks. They are a skilled group of artisans and crafts-people. The Depot also provides a variety of valuable community building efforts for Bruce Crossing and the surrounding areas. The faculty, students, and staff of Finlandia University in Hancock, and especially the library. And finally—the people of the Western U.P. who have welcomed my visits all these years. Barbara Ohata should receive a great deal of thanks for proofreading and technical assistance.

Finally, special thanks goes to Archway Publishing for shepherding this novel through the publishing process.

Thank you all once more and **SISU!** *

Ralph G. Pifer

---

*SISU—a Finnish word meaning to persist, endure, overcome—the unofficial motto of the Keweenaw Peninsula—it is frequently spotted on car bumpers.

Late October Hike to Black River Waterfalls

ABOUT THE AUTHOR

Ralph Pifer is a retired Associate Professor of Psychology and Social Science. During his career, he was recognized as "Professor of the Year" and named multiple times by students as the most influential professor in their academic careers. He has written numerous papers in the fields of Psychology and Philosophy. He continues to be active in these fields as a student and a writer. His lifelong interests in geology, nature, and photography have served him well in his explorations of Michigan's U.P. for over 40 years. He is a member of the Nature Conservancy, Sierra Club, and a number of scientific organizations. He lives in retirement in Dixon, Illinois (Ronald Reagan's hometown), with his wife, nasty cat (Ben), and ancient box turtle (Eldon).

—40 years coming to the U.P. and I still LOVE it!

Porcupine

DISCLAIMER

The author holds no financial interest in or received any reimbursement for recommendations of the sites described in this book. The contents reflect the opinions, observations, and experiences of the author, over a roughly forty year span, in Michigan's Upper Peninsula. I have done my best to present accurate information about the sites described, but no one can know or experience everything, Storms, floods, and other unforeseen events can change roads, trails, rivers, and other sites. .Your experience may differ from mine. The responsibility for safety in your travels is yours. Please be careful in your adventures. Follow all State and Park laws and regulations.

TRAVEL NOTES:

TRAVEL NOTES:

TRAVEL NOTES: